Conversations We Never Had

Conversations
We Never Had

by Jodie Armour

Caffeinated Muse Press

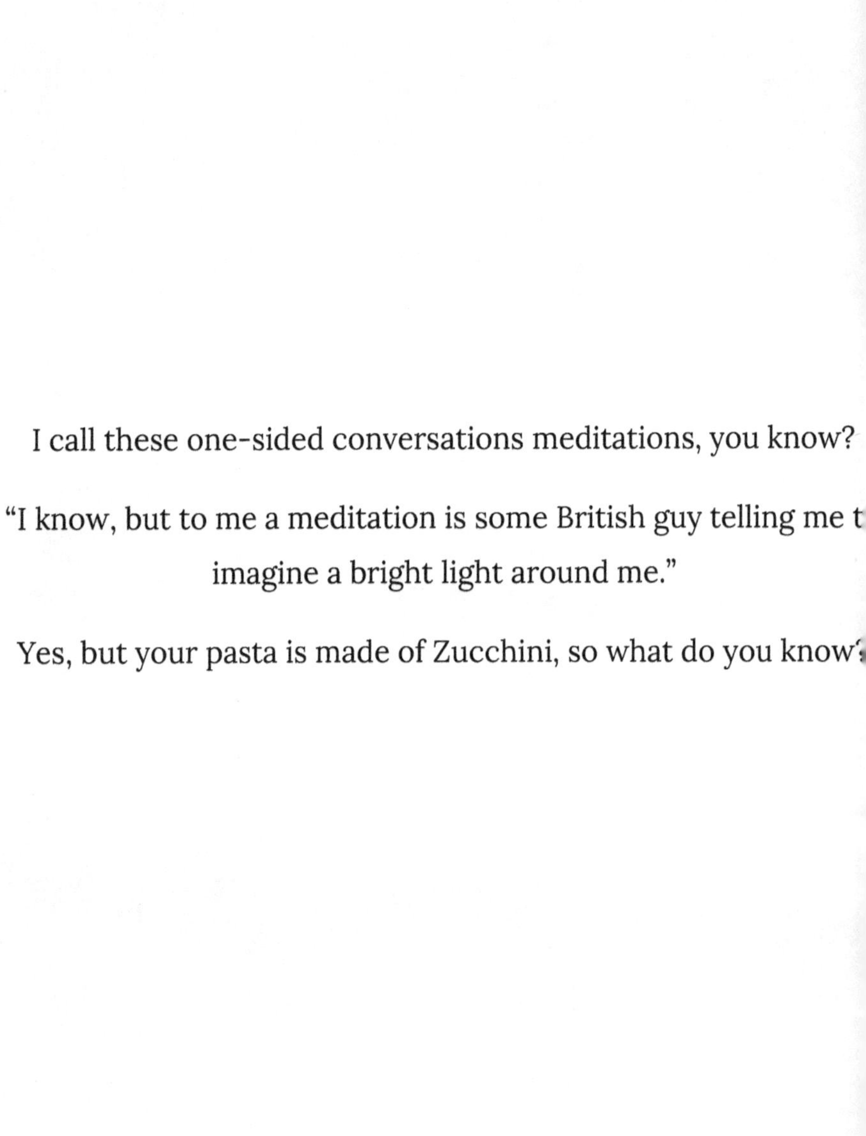

I call these one-sided conversations meditations, you know?

"I know, but to me a meditation is some British guy telling me t
imagine a bright light around me."

Yes, but your pasta is made of Zucchini, so what do you know?

"I'm going to call my autobiography Sex, Love and Poetry."

I thought it was going to be Wine, Weed and 3 A.M. ramblings.

"That was yesterday me's autobiography."

Okay, but you actually have wine, weed and 3 A.M.s.

"Ancestry changed my report. I'm no longer 26% Italian."

Are you still 31% English?

"Only 30."

I will always love you as if you are 31%.

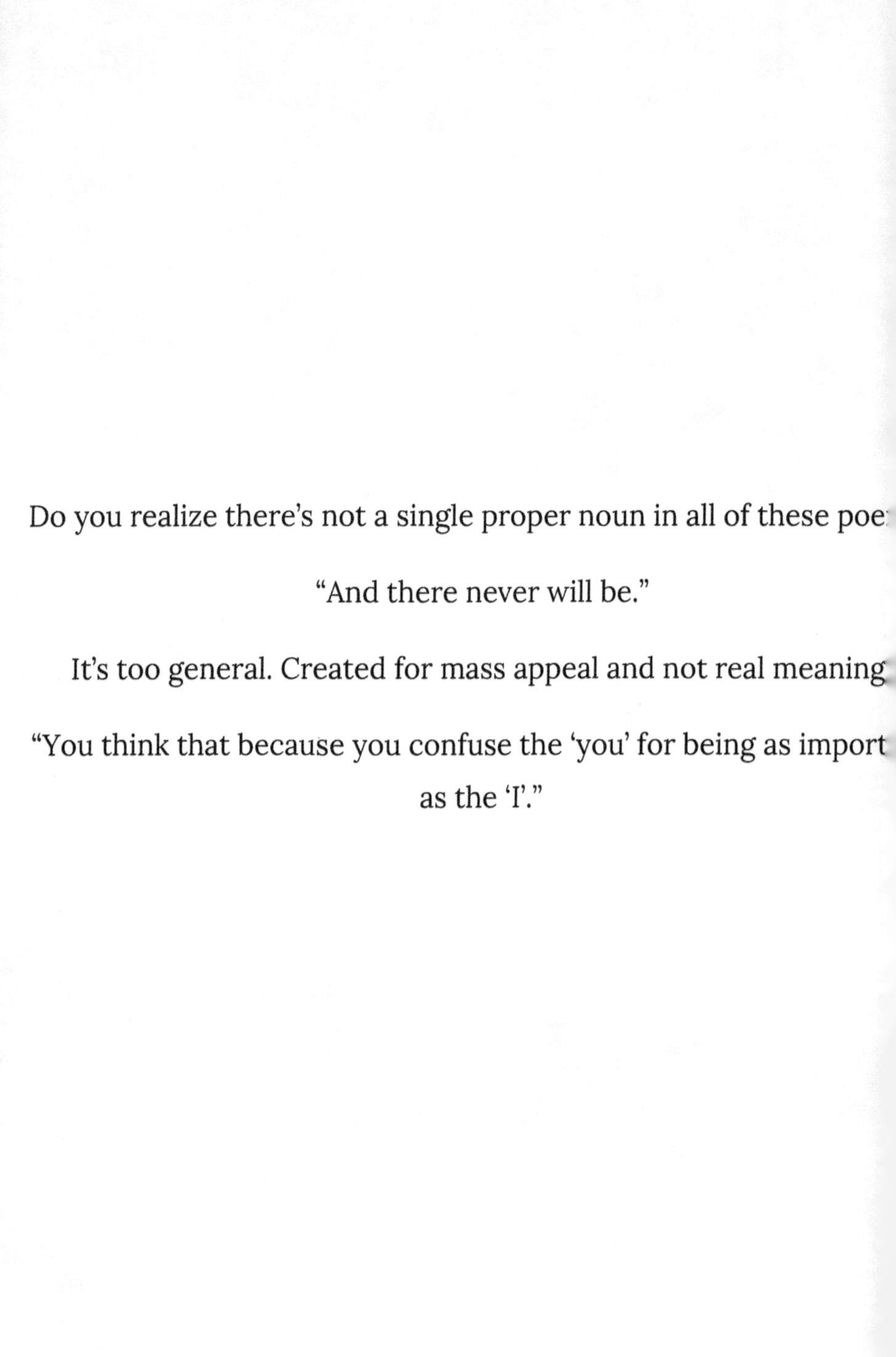

Do you realize there's not a single proper noun in all of these poe

"And there never will be."

It's too general. Created for mass appeal and not real meaning

"You think that because you confuse the 'you' for being as import

as the 'I'."

"You wrote more with me. I write more without you."

You were my muse.

"Can't I muse from afar? You do."

Let me muse over it.

"Am I insane for talking to you when you're not here?"

I wrote you 146 pages of poetry in 3 months.

"Yes, but that was just quantity not quality."

Doing the same thing and expecting a different result is insanity

"I wrote three poems today. You must be rubbing off on me."

Are they all about me?

"Yes."

That's no way to win a Pulitzer.

Unrequited? Is that what we are?

"I don't know what the fuck we are."

Which one of us is in love and which isn't?

"Depends. What day is it today?"

"The unrequited love poem is about us."

It was never unrequited. Just tremendously bad timing.

"Isn't timing what you make it?"

She says after I'm gone.

"I would have loved you for forever, you know?"

You couldn't even love me for months without getting scared.

"Forever is easier."

Forever is abstract.

If it's not about the 'you' why am I in every poem?

"I'm in them too."

But you're you. You're in everything you do.

"And you're in just these few."

"Have you written anything lately?"

A few poems.

"Are they any good?"

I wrote them.

“I should probably stop answering when you call. I mean the real y

Yeah. That guy is a dick.

“He’s just careless.”

He’s cavalier.

"Remember when you told me that you loved me so much that all 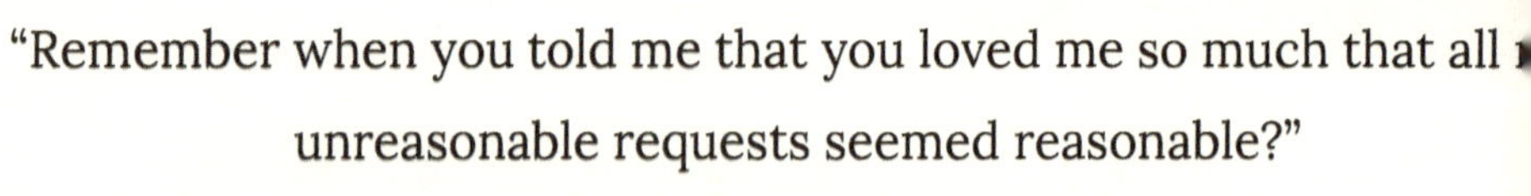
unreasonable requests seemed reasonable?"

That sounds like the poetic stuff I would have said.

"I should have told you to go to a therapist."

But you knew I didn't mean it.

"I should have never loved you."

'Tis better to have loved and lost than to spend your days posting stupid memes on Facebook.

"Thank you for rejecting me."

That's a funny thing to thank someone for.

"I was more honest and vulnerable with you than anyone."

"If I could survive your rejection, what can an editor do to me?

You built me up in your head into something that I could never live u

"A better man would have tried."

Conversations We Never Had captures the one-sided conversations we carry on with a lover only after they are gone. These poems unfold in imagined dialogue, tender and sharp and achingly human.

About the Author

Jodie Armour is a poet and English professor whose work explores love, memory, and the silences that shape our lives.

Her poetry has appeared in journals and magazines, and she is listed in the Poets & Writers Directory.

With more than fifteen years of teaching and mentoring writers, she brings a voice that is both intimate and unflinching.

Conversations We Never Had is her first chapbook, offering readers an exploration of loss, resilience, and the ways language can bridge what we cannot say.

About the Press

Caffeinated Muse Press is an independent publisher dedicated to poetry, fiction, and works that blur the boundaries between the magical and the everyday. We champion voices that speak with urgency, honesty, and imaginative power.

www.ingramcontent.com/pod-product-compliance
Lightning Source LLC
Chambersburg PA
CBHW021348060726
47591CB00006B/2213